busy baby animals

chimp

Please visit our web site at: www.garethstevens.com
For a free color catalog describing Gareth Stevens' list of high-quality books and multimedia programs, call 1-800-542-2595 (USA) or 1-800-461-9120 (Canada). Gareth Stevens Publishing's Fax: (414) 332-3567.

Library of Congress Cataloging-in-Publication Data

Johnson, Jinny.
Chimp / by Jinny Johnson; [illustrated by Ch'en-Ling; photography by Simon Murrell].
—North American ed.
p. cm. — (Busy baby animals)
ISBN 0-8368-2921-2 (lib. bdg.)
1. Chimpanzees—Infancy—Juvenile literature. [1. Chimpanzees. 2. Animals—Infancy.]
I. Ch'en-Ling, ill. II. Murrell, Simon, ill. III. Title.
QL737.P96J64 2001
599.885'139—dc21 2001020526

This North American edition first published in 2001 by
Gareth Stevens Publishing
A World Almanac Education Group Company
330 West Olive Street, Suite 100
Milwaukee, Wisconsin 53212 USA

Illustrations: Ch'en-Ling
Photography: Simon Murrell, Animal Ark
Editor: Sadie Smith
Designer: Siân Williams
Gareth Stevens editor: Katherine J. Meitner
Gareth Stevens cover design: Katherine A. Kroll

Printed in the United States of America

1 2 3 4 5 6 7 8 9 05 04 03 02 01

busy baby animals

chimp

Jinny Johnson

Gareth Stevens Publishing
A WORLD ALMANAC EDUCATION GROUP COMPANY

When chimps are very small, their mothers carry them everywhere. Bala stood up for the first time when he was six months old.

Now that Bala is bigger, he runs around on four legs. He can also stand on two legs, just like you. He is good at climbing trees, too.

At first, Bala only drank his mother's milk. Now he also eats leaves and fruit.

Bala's mother taught him to use a stick to get tasty termites out of their nest. He is not very good at it yet!

Young chimps like to play and explore. They also love to be tickled! If Bala feels scared, he runs back to his mother for a great big hug.

Chimps sleep in nests that they have built high in the trees.

Bala shares a cozy
nest with his mother.
Good night, Bala.

More about Chimps

Chimpanzees, or chimps, live in rain forests and grasslands in western and central Africa. Groups of up to 100 chimps wander the country together, searching for food. Chimps are among the few animals that use tools. They use sticks to "fish" termites out of their nests, and they use stones to crack nuts. A baby chimp drinks its mother's milk until it is four or five years old. It starts to eat solid food at the age of about three. When a female is eight or nine years old, she leaves her mother and joins a new group. Males do not leave the group in which they were born.